Working Together Against
SCHOOL VIOLENCE

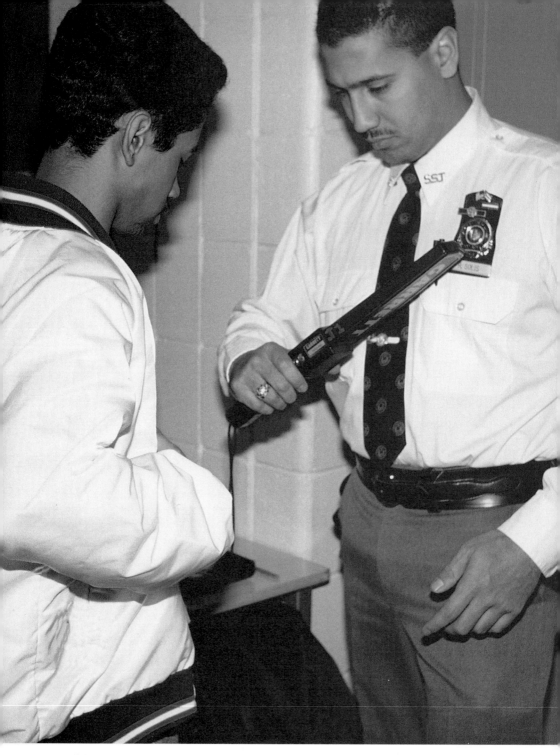

Many schools are trying to prevent violence in schools. Some schools now use metal detectors to keep guns outside and students safe on the inside.

❖ **THE LIBRARY OF SOCIAL ACTIVISM** ❖

Working Together Against

SCHOOL VIOLENCE

Sheila Klee

THE ROSEN PUBLISHING GROUP, INC.
NEW YORK

Published in 1996 by The Rosen Publishing Group, Inc.
29 East 21st Street, New York, NY 10010

First Edition

Library of Congress Cataloging-in-Publication Data

Klee, Sheila.
    Working together against school violence / by Sheila Klee.
      p. cm. — (The library of social activism)
    Includes bibliographical references and index.
    Summary: Examines the problem of violence in schools, its causes, and possible ways for teens to take action.
    ISBN 0-8239-2262-6
    1. School violence—United States—Prevention—Juvenile literature. [1. School violence. 2. Violence.] I. Title. II. Series.
    LB3013.3.K53   1996
    371.5'8—dc20   96-6917
                                                             CIP
                                                               AC

Manufactured in the United States of America.

Contents

INTRODUCTION

ALL AROUND THE NATION, IN SUBURBS,
cities, and rural areas, many students and teachers say that violent behavior in their schools is increasing. More students are involved in fights, assaults, and other hostile actions. Worse, more students are carrying and using weapons, so their fights are more dangerous. Because of violent incidents, there are days when some kids are afraid to even go to school.

Yet there is another trend that gives us hope. People are starting anti-violence programs in schools all around the country. Most young people are against violence, and many of them are leading the way to make their own schools more peaceful. They are working together with teachers, parents, and people in their communities to stop the violence around them.

Would you like to be a part of the movement against violence? You can play an important role in improving your own school and the society you live in. Success in ending violence will require the help of thousands of young people, each working in his or her own school and community and each speaking up to leaders in government and society. You can become one of these activists. You can make a real difference.

This book will help you take action. Chapters 1, 2, and 3 discuss violence and its causes. Chapters 4, 5, and 6 discuss what people are doing to stop the violence and how you can contribute or start your own project. At the end of the book are addresses and phone numbers of organizations that will help you get started or can send you more information about violence prevention.

❖ QUESTIONS TO ASK YOURSELF ❖

Many teens who become activists for social problems find that they feel stronger and more self-confident as a result of their work. As you read this book, think about how it would make you feel to be a part of the anti-violence movement. 1) Have you ever taken action against a problem in society before? 2) Do you think you would like making your school a safer place?

Many teens are exposed to scenes of violence from television shows, movies, and video games.

chapter

1

OUR VIOLENT SOCIETY

IN ORDER TO WORK EFFECTIVELY AGAINST violence in schools, we need to find its source first. Young people learn aggressive and violent behavior outside of school. They also get weapons outside of school. The violence in schools is an extension of what is happening in the rest of our society.

Violence is now a part of our everyday lives in the United States. It is part of our culture. We watch violent TV shows, go to violent movies, and rent violent videos. We play violent video games and listen to music that has violent lyrics. We glorify the violence in U.S. history. We buy toy guns and weapons for children.

These images of violence are so common that they begin to seem unreal to us. But when you hear gunfire outside your house, or when you know someone who was hurt or killed, or you get hurt yourself, violence becomes frighteningly real.

Violence is the use of force or the threat of force to harm someone physically. Every day, violence takes place in the form of fights, abuse, assaults, rapes, robbery, hate crimes, and killings.

People commit violent acts in their homes, in their friends' homes, and in their neighborhoods. There are shootings in stores and post offices. There are fights and robberies in cars and parking lots, and on public transportation. Sometimes we feel like nowhere is safe. Not even our schools.

Although the overall crime rate in the United States was lower in 1992 than in 1981, some kinds of crime are increasing again. According to the U.S. Department of Justice, violent crime grew 23 percent between 1988 and 1992. Murder and manslaughter, rape, robbery, and aggravated assault are considered violent crimes. Although adults still commit most violent crimes, in recent years, young people have become responsible for a high increase. Young people are also often the victims.

❖ YOUTH VIOLENCE ❖

The Office of Juvenile Justice and Delinquency Prevention (OJJDP) of the Department of Justice collects and analyzes data about youth crime, including both victims and offenders. This information is used by experts,

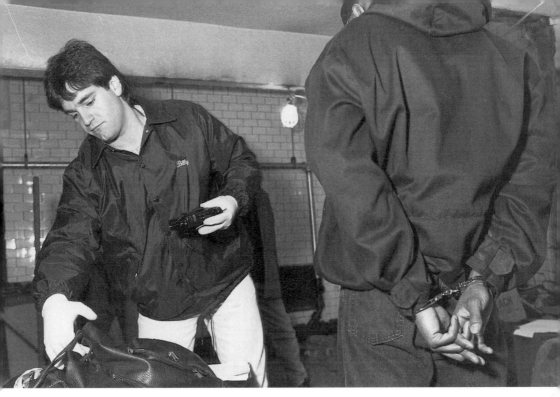

The staggering increase in the number of crimes committed by young people is frightening.

including educators, people who work with youth groups, and government officials to determine why delinquency and violence occur and how to prevent them.

Here are some findings from reports the OJJDP released in 1994 and 1995.

- More than 1.55 million crimes were committed against youths aged twelve to seventeen in 1992. This was a 25 percent increase from 1988.
- In 1992, roughly one out of thirteen young people reported being the victim of a violent crime.

- Juveniles (young people under eighteen years of age) were responsible for about one out of every five violent crimes.
- The juvenile violent crime rate rose quickly between 1988 and 1992 after having been stable for more than a decade.
- The juvenile arrest rate for weapons violations increased by 75 percent between 1987 and 1992.

A person between the ages of twelve and seventeen is more likely to be the victim of violent crime than someone over twenty-five. African American youths between fourteen and seventeen are five times more likely to be killed than whites their age. The vast majority of juvenile homicide victims were of the same race as the persons who killed them. One-quarter of juvenile murder victims are killed by other juveniles. Eighty-eight percent of offenders are boys. These figures are grim and frightening.

While some people actually face immediate violence in their lives, others are afraid because they hear stories of violence, which are often sensationalized and exaggerated on television and in newspapers. But any violence causes long-lasting psychological pain to the victims and to all of us. We lose peace of mind and quality of life. We grow afraid of each other and afraid to go outside.

Traditionally, school was one place where kids who faced violence or the fear of violence in their neighborhoods, or even in their homes, could feel safe. Now the peace is being shattered there, too. But you can play a role in helping to eliminate school violence.

❖ QUESTIONS TO ASK YOURSELF ❖

Every day, we see or hear about violent acts. 1) Have you or someone you know been a victim of violence outside of school or in school? 2) Does the fear of violence keep you from doing things or going places, in school or out of school?

chapter

2

VIOLENCE IN SCHOOLS

Conflicts between students happen in
every school. In some schools, conflicts often
lead to violence. In others, violence is rare.
Many schools fall somewhere in the middle.
They experience fighting, name-calling, and gen-
eral aggression among some of their students.
There may be a lot of classroom disruptions and
intimidation of students.

You probably know where your school fits in
this range. You know if you are more worried
about being shot in your school or about being
tripped by someone in the hall. You know if
students in your school can walk away from
fights or if they feel they have to fight when
they're challenged to protect themselves in the
future. If you go to a school which has frequent
acts of violence occurring, you are understand-
ably frightened and angry about it. But even if
you feel pretty secure in your own school, you're
probably still scared when you hear about the

growing number of violent incidents in or near schools.

❖ EXTENT OF VIOLENCE ❖

Despite incidents like these, it is hard to know just how bad school violence is in the United States. In 1994, Honeywell Inc. conducted a survey of 508 junior and senior high school teachers and students nationwide. One in three teachers and one in four students said that violence in their schools was a serious problem. In a 1994 Metropolitan Life survey, however, only about one in eight high school students said they worried about their own safety in school.

One thing most people do agree on is that school violence is getting worse. Of all the school districts that responded to a National School Boards Association survey in 1993, 82 percent said that violence in their schools had increased. Thirty-five percent said it had increased significantly. This was true whether the responding school board was in a city, a suburb, or a rural area.

❖ TYPES OF VIOLENCE ❖

According to the National School Safety Center, school incidents are most often assaults, robberies, or extortion. Assaults on students and staff can range from verbal abuse to tearing

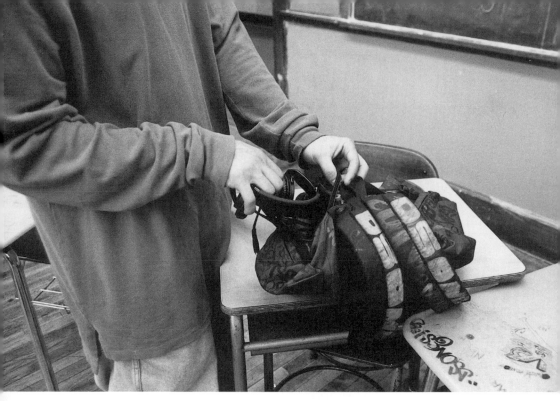

Theft is a big problem in many schools. This can be especially dangerous if threats or violence is used.

clothes, or from grabbing someone to beatings, rape, or murder. In robbery, force is used to steal something. In extortion, a student uses threats and intimidation to demand something of value, such as clothes or lunch money.

The National School Boards Association survey showed that the top five categories of violent incidents in schools in 1993 were:

- student assaults against other students
- students bringing weapons to their classrooms
- student attacks on teachers
- racial and ethnic violence
- gang-related problems

❖ VICTIMS AND OFFENDERS ❖

It is not known what percentage of students are responsible for most school violence. In one school, in Newark, New Jersey, for example, the superintendent thinks that the violence is caused by just 1 percent of the students. The head of security at the same school believes that about 5 percent of the students are responsible for the violence. In most schools, a small number of teens lead the violent behavior. Others go along with them. Many others try to protect themselves and stay away from violent teens.

❖ EFFECTS OF SCHOOL VIOLENCE ❖

Anyone can be a victim of violence in school: students, teachers, staff. That's why it is so frightening: the violence seems random, or the result of minor conflicts. Gay and lesbian youths, mentally challenged kids, or others who are seen as "different" are often victimized. Smaller and younger children are picked on. Girls are sexually harassed and insulted. Boys or girls may be attacked for unknowingly wearing gang colors or the type of hat a gang has claimed as its own. Kids may be robbed of their clothing, jewelry, or sneakers.

In an interview with *USA Today*, Secretary of Education Richard Riley said, "Violence in schools or among school-aged youths not only destroys the nation's most precious natural

resource—its children—but also creates an environment where youngsters cannot learn, teachers cannot teach, and parents are reluctant to send their offspring (kids) to class."

Instead of concentrating on their work, students in violent schools worry about what will happen in the hall between classes, in the cafeteria at lunch, or outside after school. Violence poisons the atmosphere.

❖ QUESTIONS TO ASK YOURSELF ❖

The most common kind of school violence is students assaulting other students. 1) Is this true in your school? 2) What do students fight about? 3) Are many students involved in violent or disruptive behavior?

chapter

3

WHAT CAUSES VIOLENCE?

CONFLICT AND DISAGREEMENT ARE A
normal part of life. Everyone gets angry at
another person sometimes, or upset about something that happens. And it's okay to get angry.
But why do some people respond by becoming
violent when others do not?

A lot of people have tried to find the answers
to this question, including researchers from
schools, universities, the justice system, the public health service, psychologists and psychiatrists,
and youth organizations. Different methods are
used to study the problem. For example, one
study might follow a group of children for
fifteen years, examining the conditions they live
in and seeing which kids show violent behavior
as teenagers. Then the researchers might look
for links between what happened in their lives as
children and what they do as teens. If they find
some clear links between early TV-watching and

later violence, researchers might study other children to see if they reveal the same trend. When enough of the researchers studying a problem agree that there is a connection, they can say that they have identified one contributing cause of violence.

Another method is to collect a great deal of information, called data, from and about young people who have been violent. Then researchers analyze the information to see what factors these young people have in common. They might find, for example, that many violent youths had also been victims of violence. Another study might start with victims of violence and see if they later became violent themselves. Again, if enough researchers get the same results, they can say they have identified another cause of violent behavior.

What is clear is that there is no single cause of violence. When people become violent, it is usually because of a combination of factors in their lives. Even then, it's hard to know why two people can have the same experiences and only one becomes violent.

Certain factors have been most closely linked to violent behavior.

❖ FAMILY FACTORS ❖

Family problems are one of the most important causes of violent behavior in young people.

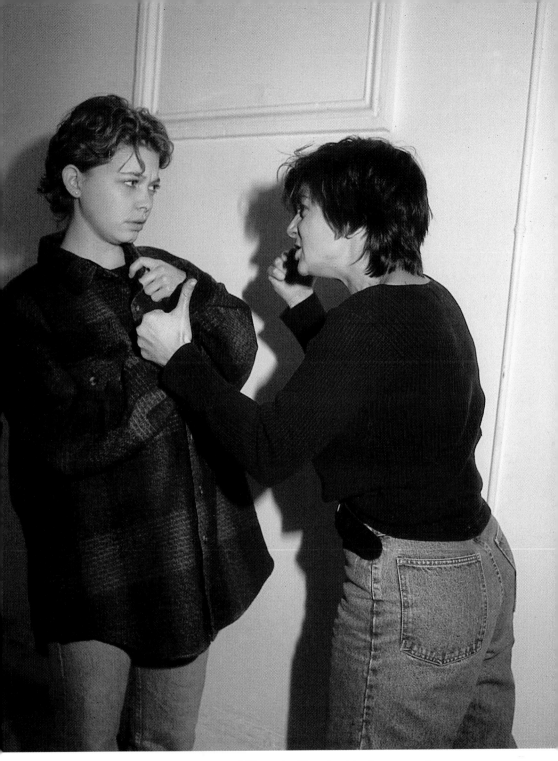

Different people respond to anger differently. Faced with the same circumstances, only some express their anger violently.

The way a child is raised has a lot to do with his or her future behavior.

Children who are abused by their families are more likely to be violent themselves and to abuse their own children. The OJJDP says that children who witness several kinds of violence in their homes, such as violence between their parents or toward them, are twice as likely to engage in violent behavior. This is a serious problem, since the study reported 1.9 million cases of child abuse in 1992.

But even parents and guardians who do not abuse their children may raise them in ways that contribute to violent behavior. Some parents spend a great deal of money on their kids but not enough time with them. Parents may not supervise their kids or give them emotional support. Some parents punish their kids severely instead of teaching them discipline. Many parents fail to teach their children how to manage anger and relate positively to other people, or even to teach them right from wrong.

For economic and social reasons, family structure has changed in recent years. There are more single parents, more divorced parents, and more teen parents. Half of all teenagers live with only one parent at some point because of divorce, separation, or the parent has remained single. Many parents, single or not, do not have the time or the skills to give their children the

stability and attention they need. This neglect can permanently damage teens.

A recent report from the Carnegie Council on Adolescent Development concluded, after a nine-year study, that the 19 million young adults in the United States (ten to fourteen-year-olds) are being neglected by the government, communities, schools, and parents at a time when they need help and support the most. According to the twenty-seven-member panel of scientists, scholars, and government officials, the result is that teens become more vulnerable to drug and alcohol abuse, violence, suicide, AIDS, teen pregnancy, and failed educations. The extent of the neglect is so bad that some teens may never be able to lead normal and productive lives.

❖ POVERTY WITHOUT HOPE ❖

Poverty is another factor in violence. According to the OJJDP, 22 percent of all juveniles were poor in 1992. The number of poor children rose by 42 percent between 1976 and 1992.

Of course, most poor people are not violent. But according to a 1993 study by the American Psychology Association (APA), violence does occur more often among the poor. The problem is not just poverty, the APA study states, but poverty without hope of improvement. It is poverty with permanently high unemployment, few chances of economic opportunity, poor health care and nutrition, and crumbling housing. It is poverty surrounded by the wealth of others, without the hope of sharing in that wealth. These are conditions that lead to the family breakdowns, dangerous neighborhoods, low self-esteem, and anger that can also be associated with violent behavior.

❖ DISCRIMINATION ❖

Racism and discrimination against groups of people in our society also foster violence, the APA study finds. First, long-term discrimination in jobs, economic opportunity, and education helps keep some minorities in much higher poverty rates, which are linked to violence. According to the OJJDP, in 1992 African American children had a poverty rate of 47 percent, and Latino children 40 percent, compared with a poverty rate of 17 percent for white children. The higher violence rate of African American youth seems to be linked to their higher poverty rates, concludes the APA. Victims of racism and discrimination also frequently have low self-esteem and anger, which, combined with other factors, can contribute to violent behavior.

❖ DRUGS AND ALCOHOL ❖

According to OJJDP, 48 percent of juveniles in

Many young people are the victims of violence, but an increasing number are also the offenders.

custody in long-term prison institutions said they had been under the influence of drugs or alcohol when they committed their offense. About 33 percent of eighth graders surveyed say they have used illegal drugs, according to the Carnegie Council. Alcohol is often involved in violent incidents, including domestic abuse.

Young people who sell drugs often carry guns and are the victims and offenders of violence related to drug dealing. Much of the individual and gang-related violence is the direct result of the drug trade. Teens who need money to buy drugs may commit crimes to get the money.

❖ GUNS ❖

According to the Children's Defense Fund, a gun kills a child in the United States every two hours. Almost fifty thousand children were killed by firearms between 1979 and 1991. Firearms are the second leading cause of death for all American teens.

Young people are not only the victims of guns but are also increasingly the offenders. According to the OJJDP, the huge increase in homicides by young people is connected to their use of guns. It's easy for many kids to buy guns or take guns that their parents keep in the house. Sometimes several youths share a gun. Young people use guns to wound and kill other people, and also to kill themselves. In fact, there is one youth suicide for every two youth murders in the United States. There are also many accidental killings with guns. Guns make violence and aggression much deadlier.

❖ TELEVISION ❖

"Viewing violence increases violence," says a report by the American Psychological Association. By mid-adolescence, teenagers have watched 15 thousand hours of television. This is more time than they have spent with their teachers. TV shows are often full of violence. Dr. Rowell Huesmann and Dr. Leonard D. Eron, who have been studying the link between

television and violence for nearly thirty-five years, told Congress in 1992 that "television violence affects youngsters of all ages, of both genders, at all socioeconomic levels, and all levels of intelligence. The effect is not limited to children who are already disposed to being aggressive, and it is not restricted to this country."

❖ STUDENT AND TEACHER OPINIONS ❖
ON CAUSES OF SCHOOL VIOLENCE

In 1994, Honeywell Inc. surveyed 250 junior and senior high school students and 258 teachers on the causes of school violence. The students said the top three causes were peer influence, the breakdown of family, and media violence. The teachers' top three reasons were the breakdown of family, media violence, and society's acceptance of violence. Obviously, some teens think that they may push each other into violent behavior. Peer pressure is a powerful force at any age, but for teenagers it is especially strong. Teens want to fit in and be popular. It can be hard for teens to resist certain behaviors, even if they don't approve of them, because they feel they have to go along with the crowd.

There is no definitive answer to the causes of violence. But there are many clear connections that let us see where violence takes root. It can start in poverty without jobs or hope for the future. It continues in families that have lost their way and cannot guide their children. It grows up in racism and discrimination that crush people's spirits and dreams. It grows out of the images on our television screens, out of the depths of drug and alcohol abuse, and out of the barrels of too many guns.

How can we free ourselves, our schools, and our society from the problems created by violence? Since we know some of the reasons behind violent behavior, we can work on the solutions.

❖ QUESTIONS TO ASK YOURSELF ❖

Causes of violence are found in the family, the individual, and in society. 1) What are some ways that problems in society can be related to family or individual problems? 2) What do you think are the most important factors in violent behavior by teenagers?

4

CAN'T SOMEONE DO SOMETHING?

THE GOOD NEWS IS THAT ALL AROUND THE country, students, teachers, parents, clergy, and concerned citizens from all parts of society are working on violence prevention.

Let's look at some of the work going on. Some projects are based in schools. Others are from local community organizations, but contribute to school safety.

GOVERNMENT POLICY

❖ NATIONAL EDUCATION GOALS ❖

In March 1994, President Bill Clinton signed the Goals 2000: Educate America Act. This act lists eight goals for American schools to achieve in order to improve education for young people. Goal 6 says: "By the year 2000, every school in America will be free of drugs and violence and will offer a disciplined environment conducive to learning."

Many people are coming together in their communities to work on violence prevention.

After setting a policy, the federal government has to help make it possible for state and local governments and schools to achieve the goal. The government does this by requiring schools to create their own plans to meet the goal and giving money, or funding, to carry out their plans. It can also withhold money if schools do not show that they are trying to meet the requirements.

For example, as one way to help schools achieve Goal 6, the law requires school districts to develop rules and a plan to keep guns out of schools and requires schools to expel students caught with guns. Schools are developing or

improving their drug programs and working on other programs to make school life safer.

❖ CRIME BILL OF 1994 ❖

In 1994, President Clinton signed a major crime bill designed to reduce crime and violence. The Crime Bill provides for more police and more prisons. It allows juveniles to be tried as adults for some violent crimes and crimes committed with guns. It also includes money for crime prevention. Some people think that being harder on criminals is the best way to deal with violence and crime. They want more emphasis placed on these areas and want less money to be provided for crime prevention.

Many strongly believe that violence prevention is a more effective strategy. The Crime Bill authorizes $6.9 billion to be spent on violence prevention programs. The money is to be spent on many local projects, including after-school programs, job creation, expansion of parks, gang deterrence, creation of youth anti-crime councils, family outreach programs, and protection of senior citizens from violence.

NONGOVERNMENTAL INITIATIVES

Young people themselves either lead or participate in hundreds of programs. The following are just a few examples.

Students trained as peer mediators help other students resolve their differences.

❖ RESOLVING CONFLICT CREATIVELY ❖ PROGRAM

The largest conflict resolution program in the country is the Resolving Conflict Creatively Program, or RCCP. About 150,000 students and 5,000 teachers in 325 schools use RCCP.

RCCP helps make "peaceable schools" by involving everyone in the school district in the plan—students, teachers, administrators, and parents. Everyone learns better ways to manage anger, solve problems, and understand others.

RCCP uses classroom lessons and trains teachers, administrators, and parents. It sets up *peer mediation* programs to teach these skills to teens. In peer mediation, students are trained to help other students resolve their conflicts peacefully. When two or more kids are arguing or fighting, they take the dispute to a student mediator. The mediator helps them work out a peaceful solution that satisfies both sides. They learn to listen to each other, to express their feelings constructively, and to respect both points of view without feeling that somebody has to win or lose.

Educators for Social Responsibility (ESR) is the group that coordinates RCCP. The program is put into effect in an entire school district, and everyone must participate for it to succeed. For schools that cannot make the commitment to the complete plan, ESR has shorter programs. These programs can also help in violence prevention by offering one-day workshops for teachers or parents, or by inviting speakers to come to schools.

❖ YFJ AND NICEL ❖

Youth for Justice (YFJ) is a program funded by OJJDP. It uses law-related education to help teens confront issues such as drug and alcohol abuse, crime, and violence. YFJ develops materials to use in classrooms, trains teachers in law education, holds programs for students, and helps students get involved in community service to help other people. The program is based on the idea that young people become less violent and more productive when they understand their legal rights and responsibilities. One program which YJF sponsors is Youth Summits.

Youth Summits is a program where young people hold major conferences about violence and related issues. They discuss their opinions with adult leaders and other teenagers, and plan anti-violence projects to carry out themselves. In 1995, more than 10,000 students, teachers, and others attended summits in forty-seven states, Washington, DC, and Puerto Rico. State governments and state bar associations (professional groups for lawyers) have helped to support these summits.

The National Institute for Citizen Education in the Law (NICEL) is another organization that

Many programs are targeting young children to teach them about violence prevention.

works in partnership with YFJ to help teens. NICEL is a nonprofit organization that teaches teens about law and democracy. The following are two programs sponsored by NICEL.

The Teens, Crime, and Community Program. An education and action program, it teaches students to prevent violence and manage conflict through a curriculum and community service.

Conflict Management/Mediation Program. This program is aimed at teaching teens peaceful methods of resolving conflict without using violence. NICEL also teaches teens conflict-resolution skills. Teachers can also learn these skills from NICEL. These teachers can then incorporate what they have learned into their classes and teach the skills to their students.

❖ SAFE START CAMPAIGN ❖

The Safe Start Campaign is cosponsored by the Children's Defense Fund (CDF) and the Black Community Crusade for Children (BCCC). The Campaign works to prevent violence against children by using programs, education, religious mobilization, and political action.

Cease Fire, a national public education effort against gun violence, is one of Safe Start's programs. Another is the annual Day of Action Against Violence, on April 4. On the Day of Action in 1994, students in New York held a march against violence through the neighborhoods around their schools. The Safe Start Campaign is also working on training local branches to take similar actions such as establishing safe corridors, or safe routes to and from schools for children, and getting guns out of the community.

❖ GIRLS INCORPORATED ❖

Girls Incorporated has a national program to prevent violence against girls. It sponsors Project Bold to help girls learn to have healthy, respectful relationships, to develop conflict-resolution skills, and to learn self-reliance, including self-defense. In one program, girls learn how to confront sexual harassment in school and elsewhere. In another, girls learn to organize against violence, including gang violence and date and acquaintance rape. Nationwide, about 350,000 kids currently participate in Girls Inc.

❖YOUTH AS RESOURCES❖

Youth As Resources (YAR) is a program of the National Crime Prevention Council. YAR believes that by helping others, young people improve their communities and at the same time lower their own risk of being involved in violence, in school and outside. YAR has many local programs based in schools, Boys and Girls Clubs, public housing authorities, and parks and recreation departments. To participate in YAR, kids identify needs in their communities and design projects to meet them. YAR helps provide funding and adult support. So far, more than 40,000 young people have participated in projects through Youth As Resources, including:

- helping children at a women's shelter
- helping senior citizens repair their homes
- helping younger children with their homework
- creating a community fitness trail
- helping homeless people

Many schools are also trying to educate teens on how to prevent dating violence.

- helping people with AIDS
- constructing a playground

❖ TEEN DATING VIOLENCE PROJECT ❖

The Teen Dating Violence Project in Austin, Texas, helps boys and girls learn to have safe and healthy dating relationships and to prevent dating violence. It is a program sponsored by the Center for Battered Women. Speakers visit schools to talk to teens about dating violence. Boys and girls who are in violent relationships participate in support groups to develop the knowledge, skills, and assertiveness to have safe, respectful relationships. The teens also help educate other kids on the right and wrong way to communicate in a relationship. They also organize projects, such as role-playing over the school PA system. Centers for battered women in other areas of the country can often help teens find speakers and other resources on dating violence.

❖ MEDIA VIOLENCE ❖

The National Foundation to Improve Television (FIT) raises public awareness of the effects of TV violence. It works to get businesses not to advertise their products during violent shows. FIT also tries to put legal restrictions on the broadcasting of violent programs during the time of day when children watch TV the most. Teens can use FIT's action strategy tips:

- Call your local TV station when it airs a violent scene or show that you object to, then follow up with a letter.
- Send copies of your letter to your representative in Congress and to the Federal Communications Commission (FCC).
- Write to advertisers to complain if they advertise on violent programs, and compliment them for good choices.

The Center for Media Literacy is another group that works against TV violence. Their mission is to make people active viewers of TV, movies, and other media. They do this by helping them understand the images, words, and sounds used by the media. In 1995, the center published "Beyond Blame: Challenging Violence in the Media," a guide for young people and parents about reducing violence in the media.

❖ SAFE SCHOOLS WEEK ❖

Safe Schools Week, usually the third week of October each year, is sponsored by the National School Safety Center. To participate in their own schools, students can start projects such as a buddy system for older students to help younger or new students in school. Here are some other things students can do:

- Start a program to invite parents to visit school regularly.
- Lobby your school or district to get students appointed to the school board.
- Reach out to the businesses and churches in your community to involve them in making your school safer.

Other national and local organizations also sponsor special anti-violence weeks in which kids are invited to participate. The national YWCA had the first annual Week Without Violence in 1995. You can participate through your local YWCA.

❖ ACTIVISM 2000 PROJECT ❖

"Act now and wake up, decision-makers. Your ideas and involvement are desperately needed," says Wendy Shaetzel Lesko, Executive Director of the Activism 2000 Project: Encouraging Youth Initiative Through Participation. Activism 2000 encourages kids to design their own projects to help change society and make adults think. The group offers a series of free bulletins on how to research, create, and publicize your project. Call their toll-free hot line, (800) KID-POWER, to discuss your project and to receive a listing of their free or low-cost publications.

Many people, both teens and adults, are working together to prevent school violence.

They work in the hopes that things can be turned around.

These efforts are a way to build awareness and education. They are a way to make schools a little safer every day. Students are among the leaders in this growing movement. You can be a part of it.

❖ QUESTIONS TO ASK YOURSELF ❖

The federal government has established laws to work against youth violence, both through increased punishment measures and more prisons and through violence prevention projects, such as after-school programs. 1) Which approach do you think is more useful? 2) How can citizens influence government decisions about violence prevention? 3) Which of the non-governmental programs we have discussed do you think would fit your school's problems?

chapter

5

STUDENTS TAKE ACTION

YOU MAY BE INSPIRED BY SOME OF THE
groups and teens we have discussed. But you
may find it hard to create your own project.
Here are some ideas to help you get going.

❖ GET STARTED ❖

First, you need to identify the problems in
your school. You can do this alone, or in a group.
Then sit down and discuss them with other students to be sure that you have an accurate pic-
ture of your school's situation. Write down all
the answers you or your group come up with.

- What kinds of violence and disruptive
  behavior happen in and around your
  school? Arguments, harassment, fights,
  fights with weapons, classroom disruption?
- Are the conflicts over personal disputes,
  race and culture, boy-girl relations, drugs,
  student/teacher problems, or other issues?

If violence is a problem in your school, you and your friends can discuss the problems and try to come up with options that can stop the violence.

- Do the same kinds of disputes occur in school as in the community, or are they different in school?
- Are many students involved or just a few?
- Where do the incidents occur, or where are students afraid to go—is it the rest rooms, hallways, playground, parking lot, school grounds, classrooms, cafeteria, or on the way to and from school?
- What kind of violence or disruption would you like to focus on first?
- What do you think are the causes of that kind of behavior?
- What would help people stop that behavior?
- What could you do to help?

❖ GET SMART ❖

Find out more about the kinds of behavior you have identified and their causes. The more knowledge you have, the better you will be able to recognize good solutions, and to create change in your school and society.

Ask a librarian in your school or public library for help in finding some of the books listed in the "For Further Reading" section in the back of this book. Also, ask him or her to suggest other books for you to read. Contact the organizations in the back of this book and ask for information about what they do and their publications and video listings. Order the free

The library is a good place to turn to for help or further information on what you can do to prevent violence in your school.

ones. You can get a lot of information and some good ideas this way. Ask your librarian or teachers if your school can obtain some of the materials that are not free. Ask the organizations if they have reduced rates for students.

❖ GET CONNECTED ❖

You are not alone in wanting peace. And you don't have to work against violence alone. In fact, you will find strength and support by working with others.

Belonging to groups in your school and community will help you to make contacts with all kinds of people. These people may be able to help you with your ideas on violence prevention. And they may very well want and need your support for their own ideas or for existing projects.

❖ SPEAK UP ❖

Your ideas and opinions must be heard if school violence is to be ended. The programs and projects and lessons will not work unless your and your fellow students' ideas and experiences are included in their design and the way they are carried out. A lot of successful plans will be carried out almost completely by students.

Make yourself known at school. What teachers and administrators know you by name? How about the guidance counselor? Introduce yourself to the principal. Go with friends to do this if it is easier. Ask your school leaders for regular opportunities to talk with them about school problems such as violence.

You may not be old enough to vote now, but you will be at eighteen. When you are old enough, register to vote. Then vote in the first elections that come up—local, state, or national. Vote for people who will help improve the schools and your community.

❖ SPEAK OUT ❖

Speaking out to other teens against violence

can be harder than speaking up to adults. You may worry about what your peers will think of you. You may fear that you won't be accepted. But someone has to tell the truth about violence.

Teens listen to their peers. Teens understand what other teens are going through. If you can find the courage to speak out, you can have a positive impact on others. You may be surprised to find out how many other students agree with you.

This doesn't mean that you have to make speeches in the halls or get in the middle of fights. But you can speak out against violence in class discussions. You can refuse to take part in hateful conversations or in insults or harassment. If you think the latest song, music video, or movie is too violent or too sexist, talk about it with your friends.

You can get together with other students. Ask the school to start an anonymous method for kids to report when they know someone is carrying a weapon or planning a violent act. Adults often don't know what's going on. A reliable system that lets teens safely and anonymously report violence by phone or message can help everyone avoid trouble.

❖ TAKE ACTION ❖

Once you have identified the problem you want to take action on, learned more about it,

If you have been hurt, or know of others who have been hurt by violence in your school, speak to a teacher or the principal about your ideas on violence prevention.

and joined a group or gotten a few friends or a class together, you can create a project.

Talk to each other about different possibilities. Look at the examples in this book and in other books. Choose a project that seems right for you and your school. Be realistic about how much time you can put in and how much money you will need to raise. You may want to get help from teachers and advisers in putting your project into action.

❖ WALK THE WALK ❖

You must also take *personal* responsibility for your character and behavior.

Don't just talk the talk about ending violence and conflict. Try to remove violence from your own life wherever possible. You can turn off the violence on your television (or at least change the channel). You can choose your friends. You can do community work and help others. You can put as much distance as possible between you, drugs, alcohol, and weapons.

You can't make your family give you the support and attention you need, or make them stop fighting if they are unable to do so. But you can ask them to try, and you can find other caring adults to include in your life. You can ask for help through your religious group or your YMCA or a group such as the Big Brothers/Big Sisters program.

You are a role model for all the children younger than you. Be a good one. They are already learning about violence and fighting. Show them, by how you live, that there is another way.

❖ QUESTIONS TO ASK YOURSELF ❖

In most schools, the majority of kids want a peaceful atmosphere. 1) Is that true in your school? 2) How many of those students would actually be willing to work on a project against violence? 3) Do you think a small group, or several small groups, could make a difference?

chapter

6

NUTS AND BOLTS

LET'S SEE HOW SOME TEENS ACTUALLY worked on a project in a high school in the Northeast. This is the nuts and bolts of a project in progress.

This high school is in a small industrial city where there are many immigrants from other countries. There has been a lot of conflict between kids from different backgrounds in the school. There has also been conflict among the adults in the community.

A typical incident in the school is a minor fight between two students, usually boys. While arguing, they turn to making racist insults against each other. Once that starts, all the other teens feel that they have to side with their cultural group against everyone in the other group. Sometimes fights erupt between dozens of students after school. Other times, the conflict and tension seem to hang over everybody in school for days before things quiet down—until the next time. Students start thinking in "us" and "them" terms, even if they have friends from other backgrounds. And some teens have started carrying weapons to school, like box cutters.

The school administration decides to try to improve multicultural understanding. The principal selects some students from various cultural groups to take part in regular meetings in order to help them understand one another. Those teens get along better with each other, but the change does not spread through the school.

Some concerned teachers start a peer mediation program to help students resolve their conflicts peacefully. They choose some students to be trained as mediators, people who listen to both sides of an argument. The program works pretty well when students use it, but usually, they only go when the school gives them a choice between mediation and suspension.

Then a teacher hears about some $1,000 grants that the state's attorney general's office is giving to students who start Youth Against Racism Groups in their schools. The groups are able to use the money for any projects that will educate students about racism and violence in school. The teacher announces this in a number of classes. When fourteen students from different cultures say they want to do it, the teacher helps them apply for the grant and agrees to be their adviser when they receive it.

First, the students get together and start talking. They decide they need to make it popular to be against racism and the fights racism is causing in their school. They have a number of meetings about what to do. Everyone has a different idea. Some are too complicated, and some are too expensive.

Finally they agree to write a pledge for students to take. When a person signs a pledge card, he or she makes a personal commitment not to be racist in word or behavior, to speak out against racism by others, and to respect people of other cultures. Then, using their grant money, the group members have the pledge cards printed.

Every lunch period for a week, they set up tables in the cafeteria and ask students to sign the pledge. Some students are suspicious at first. Only ten sign up the first day. But every day, the group posts the new pledge cards on the bulletin board. People start stopping by to see who is signing up. By the end of the week, 300 students have made the commitment to respect other people and not to be racist. Some new students also join the group and come to the next weekly meeting.

Next, several members send away for more information about conflict resolution. They ask the teachers who started the mediation program in their school to speak with their group. Then the group decides to try to get the school to expand the peer mediation plan. They ask that everyone in the school be trained in conflict resolution and mediation techniques. They also want a say in the choice of peer mediators. The school administration agrees to their

The first step to violence prevention is to make others aware of the problem.

ideas in principle. It looks for funding to expand the program.

Next, the students appoint a committee of four members of different cultural backgrounds. They send the committee to a meeting with the principal and some teachers. The committee requests that more materials about their four cultures be included in classes. They say that some students would be happy to teach their teachers about the students' cultures so that everyone will understand each other better. Some of the students also say that their parents would be willing to talk to the teachers more often if the school could get translators for parents who don't speak English. The teachers are enthusiastic. The school is considering this request too.

Finally, the youth group decides to plan an anti-violence and anti-racism campaign for the next year. They want to target the new freshman class. Using ideas from materials they get from other groups, one committee starts writing a skit to perform in assembly. They get a teacher with acting experience to be their drama coach. Another committee starts working on a poster with an anti-racism message. A printing shop in the neighborhood agrees to donate its services to print the poster.

Finally, the Youth Against Racism Group decides to evaluate its success at the end of each school year. It will try to see what impact it has had on students' attitudes and on racist fights in school. The adviser will help them write a questionnaire and also to create a method to keep track of racist incidents at the school.

If violence is a problem in your school, you can do something about it. Get together with your friends and come up with ideas, talk to your teachers or parents—take action. As you can see, taking action and getting results require hard work and cooperation. Sometimes things proceed smoothly, but often they hit problems or slow down for a while. It can also be fun and interesting to get involved. Working together, students can combine their energy and enthusi-

56

SCHOOL VIOLENCE

asm and ideals. They can learn to work as a team, and they can learn to be leaders. They can help to stop the violence in their schools.

❖ QUESTIONS TO ASK YOURSELF ❖

Schools often find that the most successful anti-violence programs are the ones led by students, with adults in a strong supporting role. 1) Are there any violence-prevention programs already in place in your school or in other schools near you? 2) Do students participate? Do the programs work? 3) How could the programs be made better?

GLOSSARY

abuse (v.) To injure or damage by physical or verbal action.

aggression Actions intended to control another; hostile behavior.

anonymous Not revealing name or identity.

assault Violent attack against another person.

delinquency State of neglect or violation of the law.

expel To force someone out of an organization or school.

gender Sex, as male or female.

hate crime Offense committed against a person or group solely because of hatred toward the victim or victims.

homicide The killing of a person by another.

instability Lack of mental or emotional balance or stability.

intimidation Creating fear through threat or use of force.

manslaughter The unlawful killing of a person without malice toward him or her.

mediator One who tries to settle disputes between parties who have differences.

mobilization To put into action or movement.

sensationalize To make an event of special interest by stressing the ugly details.

sexual harassment Persistent annoyance by sexual remarks or advances.

socioeconomic Having to do with both social and economic matters.

Organizations to Contact

Activism 2000 Project
P.O. Box E
Kensington, MD 20895
(800) KID-POWER
e-mail: ACTIVISM@aol.com

Big Brothers/Big Sisters of America
230 North 13th Street
Philadelphia, PA 19107
(215) 567-7000
e-mail: bbbsa@aol.com

Center for Media Literacy
1962 South Shenandoah Street
Los Angeles, CA 90034
(213) 931-4177
e-mail: cml@earthlink.net

Children's Defense Fund
25 E Street NW
Washington, DC 20001
(202) 628-8787
web site: http://www.tmn.com/cdf/index.html

Educators for Social Responsibility
23 Garden Street
Cambridge, MA 02138
(617) 492-1764
e-mail:esrmain@igc.apc.org

Girls Inc.
30 East 33rd Street
New York, NY 10016-5394
(212) 689-3700
e-mail:hn3578@handsnet.org

National Crime Prevention Council
1700 K Street NW
Washington, DC 20006
(800) NCPC-911

National Foundation to Improve Television
60 State Street
Boston, MA 02109
(617) 523-5520

National School Safety Center
4165 Thousand Oaks Boulevard
Westlake Village, CA 91362
(805) 373-9977

**Resolving Conflict Creatively Program,
   National Center**
163 Third Avenue
New York, NY 10003
(212) 387-0225
e-mail:rccp@igc.apc.org

Youth for Justice
National Law-Related Education Resource Center
American Bar Association
541 North Fairbanks Court
Chicago, IL 60611
(312) 988-5735

IN CANADA

Canadian Civil Liberties Association
#403, 229 Yonge Street
Toronto, ON M5B 1N9
(416) 363-0321

**Canadians Concerned About Violence in
  Entertainment (C-CAVE)**
167 Glen Road
Toronto, ON M4W 2W8
(416) 961-0853

Victims of Violence National Inc.
Unit 2, 220 Mulock Drive
Newmarket, ON L3Y 7V1
(416) 836-1010

FOR FURTHER READING

Burch, Joann J. *Marian Wright Edelman: Children's Champion*. Brookfield, CT: Millbrook Press, 1994.

Canada, Geoffrey. *Fist, Stick, Knife, Gun: A Personal History of Violence in America*. Boston: Beacon Press, 1995.

Children's Defense Fund. "The State of America's Children Yearbook." Washington, D.C., 1995.

Lesko, Wendy Schaetzel. *No Kidding Around: America's Young Activists Are Changing the World and You Can Too*. Kensington, MD: Information USA, Inc., 1992.

Lewis, Barbara A. *The Kid's Guide to Social Action: How to Solve the Social Problems You Choose—and Turn Creative Thinking into Positive Action*. Minneapolis: Free Spirit Press, 1991.

Miller, Maryann. *Working Together Against Gun Violence*. New York: Rosen Publishing, 1994.

INDEX

ABOUT THE AUTHOR
Sheila Klee is an editor and writer in New York City.

PHOTO CREDITS: Cover photo, p. 30 © Impact Visuals/Marilyn Humphries; p. 2 © Impact Visuals/ Tom McKitterick; p. 8 by Kim Sonsky; p. 11 © Impact Visuals/F.M. Kearney; p. 16 by Yung-Hee Chia; p. 21 by John Novajosky; p. 25 © Impact Visuals Andrew Lichenstein; p. 32 by Michael Brandt; p. 35 © Image Bank/Richard Pan; p. 38 © Image Bank/Kasala; pp. 44, 46 by Lauren Piperno; p. 49 by Sarah Friedman; p. 54 by Katherine Hsu.

PHOTO RESEARCH: Vera Amadzadeh

DESIGN: Kim Sonsky